ART AROUND THE WORLD

At the time of Renoir

THE IMPRESSIONIST ERA

© Aladdin Books Ltd 2001

Designed and produced by
Aladdin Books Ltd
28 Percy Street
London W1P 0LD

*First published in
Great Britain in 2001 by*
Franklin Watts
96 Leonard Street
London EC2A 4XD

ISBN 0 7496 4412 5

*A catalogue record for this
book is available from the
British Library.*

Editor
Liz White

Design
Flick, Book Design and Graphics

Picture Research
Brian Hunter Smart

Printed in the U.A.E.

ART AROUND THE WORLD

At the time of
Renoir

Antony Mason

FRANKLIN WATTS
LONDON • SYDNEY

Contents

Renoir was one of the founders of Impressionism, a new and exciting way of painting and looking at the world that burst onto the art scene in France in the 1870s. At that time, many of the most famous artists painted elaborate, polished and detailed paintings, usually on historical or religious subjects.

The Impressionists wanted to take art in a different direction, painting the real, living world they saw around them. They painted quickly to catch the mood at a certain moment on a certain day.

At first the public scorned their work as sketchy and unfinished. But before long, Impressionism was recognised as an important trend in modern art. In fact, the story of modern art could be said to begin with Impressionism.

A detail from Harvest (1851), by Daubigny.

Response to Landscape

During the early part of the 19th century, people began to see the landscape in a new way. Influenced by the Romantic poets and painters, they looked to see how the mood, the weather and the sunlight in a landscape affected their emotions. In France, the Barbizon School of artists – which was led by Théodore Rousseau (1812-67) and included Charles-François Daubigny (1817-78) – painted pictures purely of the landscape. This was at a time when most other artists were still using landscape only as a backdrop to the main scene in the painting.

Painting from nature

The artists in the Barbizon School placed great emphasis on nature, and made sketches in watercolour and oil outside. But they usually painted the finished canvas back in the studio. Nonetheless the sketches brought a new sense of freshness to their work.

This approach to landscape was new in France, but its origins could be traced back to England. The members of the Barbizon School were greatly influenced by earlier English painters, such as John Constable (1776-1837) and Richard Parkes Bonington (1802-28). Both of them exhibited in the 1824 Paris 'Salon' (the great public exhibitions of art, held almost every year, and organised by the French Royal Academy of Painting). Bonington, like the Barbizon School artists, made quick

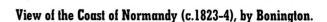

View of the Coast of Normandy (c.1823-4), by Bonington.

sketches in watercolour or oil paint outside. These show little detail, but capture a feel for the landscape.

A similar movement developed in the USA. At this time, most of the central and western parts of the country were virtually unknown to eastern Americans. But painters from the Rocky Mountain School, such as Albert Bierstadt (1830-1902), showed the rest of America the magnificent landscapes of the West.

Buffalo Trail: The Impending Storm (1869), by Bierstadt. When this painting was made, the vast buffalo herds on the plains of central USA were being destroyed by hunters with rifles, who arrived on the newly-built railways.

Around the World
Japan

Japan remained virtually closed to the outside world from 1639 until the 1850s. During this time Japanese artists developed a highly distinctive kind of painting and woodblock print known as Ukiyo-e, pictures of 'the floating world'. The appreciation of landscape, or 'views', formed part of this 'floating world'.

Inume Pass in Kai Province (c.1829-33), by Katsushika Hokusai.

Mountain views

Some of the most famous landscape prints of this period were made by Katsushika Hokusai (1760-1849). His prints have a remarkable sense of composition, with a mixture of boldness and simplicity. His prints were transported abroad and it is thought that Cézanne's later serial images of Mont Sainte-Victoire may have been inspired by Hokusai's many prints of Mount Fuji.

Realism

The development of modern art is largely the story of artists reacting to the established ways of painting. Before the mid-1800s, only certain subjects were considered suitable and 'noble' enough for art – history, religion, Classical mythology, beautiful or impressive landscapes and idealised portraits that emphasised the best features of the sitter. In the 1850s, a set of artists reacted to this approach to art, and began to paint pictures of real life – of modern, ordinary people, labourers, villagers, peasants working in the fields. The movement was called 'Realism', and it shocked many people in the world of fine art.

Life as it is lived

The leading Realist in France was Gustave Courbet (1819-77), the son of a farmer and a painter of great energy. He painted pictures with titles like *The Stone-Breakers* and *The Peasants at Flagey*. His *Burial at Ornans* is a huge picture depicting the sombre misery of a village funeral – not the sort of subject at all that conventional art-lovers expected.

Bonjour, Monsieur Courbet (1854), by Courbet.

There were social and political messages in Courbet's work. He dismissed most of the art of his day as frivolous. He wanted people to see the hardships of ordinary, everyday life, and he wanted to paint the world without any romanticised interpretation. In addition, Courbet saw himself as an 'artist-hero', taking risks for the good of humanity. His painting *Bonjour, Monsieur Courbet* reflects this rather inflated view of himself: he portrays an art collector and a patron respectfully greeting him as he heads off to do a day's painting.

Around the World
USA

French Realism had a major impact on one of the USA's greatest painters, Thomas Eakins (1844-1916). Born and brought up in Philadelphia, he studied in Paris from 1866 to 1870. Back home he taught at the Pennsylvania Academy of Fine Arts, where he caused controversy by insisting that his pupils drew from live nude models so they would understand the human body.

The Oarsmen (The Shreiber Brothers) (1874), by Thomas Eakins. Many of Eakins' most famous paintings feature bathing and boating scenes.

Real bodies

Eakins' work was not popular until the final years of his life. His subjects, such as boxing matches and doctors at work – including the gory details of surgery – were too frank for the art-buying public. His portraits were likewise very realistic, and unflattering, but they have an honesty about them that recalls the portraits of the great Dutch master Rembrandt.

In 1855 Courbet organised an exhibition in Paris called 'Le Réalisme', underlining his new approach to art. Later his work became less political, but he always insisted on painting what he saw, and refused to invent anything from his imagination. Reality was beautiful enough in itself, he believed.

Another French artist called Jean-François Millet (1814-75) was painting peasant scenes from his own region of Normandy. He wanted to show the beauty as well as the hardships of ordinary country life, which he depicted in warm, soft-focus colours.

The Gleaners (1857), by Millet.

The Path to Impressionism

An important technical development in painting took place in the 1840s: the invention and manufacture of tubes of oil paint. Before this, painters had to mix their own paints. But now, manufacturers could produce a range of colours in small, portable tubes. This made it much easier for artists to paint outside, in the open air, or 'en plein air', as the French put it. Over the next 20 years or so, landscape artists began to take their easels outside and to paint directly in front of the landscape.

Plein air painting

Some artists still only made their sketches out of doors, and did the finished oil-colour painting in the studio. This was the case with the Dutch artist Johan Barthold Jongkind (1819-91), a friend of the Barbizon School artists in the 1840s and 1850s, and famous for his pictures of coasts and ports. But he painted his watercolours outside, often working extremely rapidly to try to catch the changing light.

Boating (1874), by Manet. Manet's later paintings show an Impressionist influence in the use of lighter colours.

In 1858 Jongkind met Eugène Boudin (1824-98). Boudin was a great enthusiast for plein air painting. He is best known for the many pictures he made of the coast of northern France, often showing people on holiday. His canvases were quite small, and he worked rapidly, with thick dabs of paint, so the main theme is the mood of the scene rather than details. 'Everything that is painted directly on the spot always has a force, a power, a vivacity of touch that cannot be re-created in the studio,' he wrote.

Outrage

Another major artist of the 1860s was Edouard Manet (1832-83), a highly skilled artist working mainly in Paris. He came to fame suddenly in 1863 for a painting called *Déjeuner sur l'Herbe*. It is a picture of a picnic in a wood. However, seated beside two men in modern dress is an entirely naked woman. It was supposedly a scene from modern life, in which such behaviour would be considered highly immoral. Manet was being deliberately provocative: he was poking fun at the high ideals of official, or academic art, which limited what you could paint.

Déjeuner sur l'Herbe was one of many paintings that caused uproar at a famous exhibition in Paris in 1863. The exhibition was called the Salon des Refusés because it was especially set up to display the many paintings that had been rejected (or 'refused') by the official Salon exhibition that year.

One artist in Manet's group was Berthe Morisot (1841-95). Morisot and the others in this circle began to paint pictures of modern life in a lighter way – scenes focusing on people doing ordinary things, or enjoying themselves, boating, in the garden or dancing.

Left: The Butterfly Hunt, painted by Berthe Morisot in 1874. She was trained as an artist, but adopted a lively, sketchy style which can be traced back to Manet and Boudin.

Below: The Beach at Trouville (1864), by Boudin. Although he did not paint in all the details, Boudin's work was very accurate, catching people's movements precisely.

The Road to Versailles (1873), by Sisley.

Monet often went to paint at a pleasure resort called the La Grenouillère ('The Froggery'), on the River Seine near Paris. They liked the way the light played on water, and tried to imitate this with dabs of bright colour. But the general public did not think their paintings were much good at all. They thought they looked unfinished.

The group's work was repeatedly rejected by the official Salon exhibition in Paris, so in 1874 they organised an exhibition of their own. Most of the critics were scornful. One of them, called Louis Leroy, in referring to a painting by

Impressionism

The 1860s were an exciting time for young artists in Paris. Under the influence of painters like Jongkind, Boudin and Manet, they turned their backs on the old, formal ways of painting, as taught by the French Royal Academy. Instead, they took their paints and the canvases outdoors and tried to depict not just a scene, but the movement of the clouds, the wind in the trees, the warmth of the summer sunlight. Several of them had met at the studio of the famous art teacher Charles Gleyre (1808-74). He was rather an old-fashioned painter, but he encouraged his pupils to paint in the open air, and allowed them to develop their own styles. Among them were Claude Monet (1840-1926), Pierre-Auguste Renoir (1841-1919) and Alfred Sisley (1839-99).

Gleyre's studio closed in 1864, but the friends remained in touch, and often painted together out of doors. In the summer of 1869, Renoir and

La Grenouillère: The Bathing Place (1871-2), by Renoir.

Monet called *Impression: Sunrise*, mockingly called the artists 'Impressionists'. The artists thought the description suited their work rather well. They were, after all, trying to make impressions of the scenes they painted, not a detailed record. So Impressionism was born. A further eight Impressionist exhibitions followed; the last was in 1886.

Summer (1874), by Monet. Painted just after the first Impressionist exhibition in Paris, it shows the great sense of space and peace found in many of Monet's landscapes.

A critic of the 1876 Impressionist exhibition wrote: 'Five or six lunatics... What a terrifying spectacle this is of human vanity...'

Landscapes

There were four key figures in the Impressionist movement: Renoir, Monet, Sisley and also their older friend Camille Pissarro (1830-1903). But there were perhaps another 25 artists who were associated with it. They included Berthe Morisot, Mary Cassatt (1844-1926) and Gustave Caillebotte (1848-94).

Pissarro, Sisley and Monet are known primarily for their landscapes. Their Impressionist technique gives their landscapes a rare freshness and honesty.

Camille Pissarro was greatly influenced by the landscapes of the English painter John Constable, whose work he was able study during his stay in London in 1870-1. He was the only one of the group to participate in all eight Impressionist exhibitions, and he continued to paint in the Impressionist style more or less consistently until the end of his life. Alfred Sisley had English parents, but spent almost all his life in France, painting mainly in the Paris region.

Many of the Impressionists were poor during the 1870s, but began to have more success in the 1880s, thanks largely to their supporter, the energetic art dealer Paul Durand-Ruel.

Manorhouse at the Hermitage, Pontoise (1873), by Pissarro.

Impressionist Realism

The Impressionists did not paint historical or religious subjects, or anything that came from the imagination. In fact, they shared many of the ideas of France's greatest Realist painter Gustave Courbet. However Courbet wanted to paint the tough realities of ordinary life, while the Impressionists concentrated only on subjects that they found pleasant, beautiful or interesting. For them, this was the reality of their lives: they had no particular social message to transmit.

Industrial world

Monet was fascinated by the Paris railway station called Gare Saint-Lazare. The station was a familiar part of the Impressionists' lives: they took the train regularly to visit the suburbs and countryside around Paris. Monet made a series of paintings in and around Gare Saint-Lazare in 1876-7. This idea was considered unusual at the time. Few artists had attempted to make paintings of something so industrial and so ordinary, and just as if it were a pretty landscape. But Monet wanted to show that Impressionism could tackle any subject – a smoke-filled railway station just as much as a sun-filled wheat field.

In addition, Monet demonstrated convincingly that Impressionism could depict more than what the eye can see: these paintings also

Gare Saint-Lazare (1877), by Monet.

convey a strong sense of the noise, the smell, the energy of the trains and the busy activity of a railway station. In other words, Impressionism could portray mood very effectively. This was due to the success of the Impressionist way of applying paint, rapidly, in dabs, right across the whole canvas. Supporters of the Impressionists praised this work, calling it truly modern art.

The play of light

Fellow Impressionist Gustave Caillebotte painted scenes from Parisian life using his more precise style. He was particularly interested in the play of light on surfaces. In his famous painting *The Floor Planers* (1875), light from a window reflects off the polished floor surface, and the sweating bare backs of the workmen planing the floorboards. The subject – labourers at work – drew criticism at the 1876 Impressionist exhibition for being too realistic. Unlike most of the Impressionists, Caillebotte was wealthy. He helped the others out, lending them money and buying their paintings.

Paris: A Rainy Day (1876-7), by Caillebotte. In this highly unusual composition, Caillebotte has placed his main figures off-centre. As a result the street itself, shiny with rain, becomes the main subject of the painting.

Around the World
Belgium

Realism played a role in the development of Belgian art in the 1800s. Artists such as Jan Stobbaerts (1838-1914) painted striking images of rural life, while Hippolyte Boulenger (1837-74) painted landscapes in a rapid style that paralleled Impressionism.

A worker's life

Léon Frédéric (1856-1940) used a highly polished style to paint workers and poor families, expressing their hardships with a deep sense of compassion. There are strong elements of imagination and interpretation in his paintings, contrasting with the realism of the Impressionists, who aimed simply to record what they saw.

The Changing Ages of the Worker (1895-7), by Léon Frédéric.

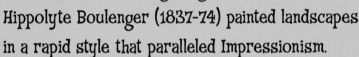

Catching the Light

Monet's interest in painting railways may have been unusual, but he was not the first. The English artist J.M.W. Turner (1775-1851) painted 'Rain, Steam and Speed: The Great Western Railway' over thirty years before Monet worked on his Gare Saint-Lazare series. During his career as a painter, Turner's landscapes had become increasingly experimental. He used colour and vigorous brushstrokes rather than detail to convey the mood of the scene. His work had a major influence on the Impressionists.

Dots and dabs

The Impressionists took Turner's experiments several stages further. They worked outside, and rapidly, busily trying to capture the light effect of a particular time of day, before it changed. They dabbed the paint on quickly and thickly, happy to leave the surface lumpy, and showing the marks left by the brush – an effect known as 'impasto'. They built up shapes with these dabs of paint, often using contrasting blocks of colour placed side by side. This can be seen in Renoir's *Landscape near Essoyes*.

Compared to traditional painting methods, this was a very different approach. Since the Renaissance, painters had tried to create rounded, three-dimensional images by carefully shading their colours, so that they blended into one another smoothly.

Landscape near Essoyes (1897), by Renoir.

16

Monet was particularly concerned with studying the changing effects of light. During the early 1890s, he worked on several series of paintings of the same subjects, designed to show just that. He made a series of paintings of Rouen Cathedral, of poplar trees and of haystacks. He would often paint the same subject many times in one day. Fifteen of the *Haystacks* paintings were exhibited together in 1891. The range of colour-effects is startling. *Haystack at Sunset* is filled with golden yellows, while the shadows turn to a fiery orange. On the other hand, *Haystacks, End of Summer* (below) is dominated by blues, giving a gentler effect; the light is clearly sharp and summery, but the reddened shadow suggests fairly intense heat.

The Impressionists developed theories about the use of colour. They achieved their dappled effect by using contrasting colours based on the colour wheel. Draw a cake with six equal slices cut into it. Paint the primary colours (red, blue and yellow) on three of the slices, leaving a blank between them. Now paint the blanks by mixing the two colours on either side: so in the blank between yellow and red you will have orange, for example. Colours on the opposite sides of the wheel are called complementary colours. For instance, orange is opposite blue – so they are complementary colours. Monet has used these two next to each other in the haystack below. Another feature of the Impressionists' paintings is the absence of black. They found black unnatural, and used blue instead.

Haystacks, End of Summer (1891), by Monet.

Monet

Impressionism lasted only a fairly short time, and the group had begun to disperse even before the last Impressionist exhibition in 1886. During the 1880s, their radical style of painting began to win wider acceptance from the general public, and they sold more paintings. Monet was able to rent and then buy a beautiful old farmhouse in Giverny in northern France, it served as his home and studio for the last 40 years of his life.

Pond at Montgeron (1876), by Monet.

Giverny

At Giverny, Monet intensified his studies of nature and landscape, both in the surrounding countryside, and in the beautiful water-gardens that he created near to the house. At first he remained true to his Impressionist style of the 1870s. However, although he had always been very keen to promote the idea of painting outdoors, he now began to bring his work into his studio (a converted barn) to finish it off – something that he was reluctant to admit to at first.

The Waterlily Pond: Harmony in Pink (1900), by Monet.

Monet travelled extensively, painting vigorously everywhere he went, but back at home, his garden began to feature more and more as the subject of his paintings, and after 1899 the waterlily pond became his favourite subject. He made a series of studies of the 'Japanese' footbridge that he had built over the pond. These paintings still show a surface broken up with dabs of complementary colours, in true Impressionist style. But they begin also to reflect a key theme that occupied Monet in the last decades of his life: peace and contemplation.

Waterlilies

Gradually, Monet was drawn to the light-effects on the surface of the pond itself, and the reflection of the sky in the water. Increasingly, his paintings became more like a field of colour, with just a few details – the lilies and their leaves – to remind us what we are looking at. Very few painters had ever attempted to make whole paintings of such a subject. Monet was moving towards abstract art.

Monet's eyesight, however, began to fail, and by about 1915 he had begun to lose his sense of colour. This was restored in 1923, when he had a successful cataract operation on his eyes. By this time, Monet was one of France's most celebrated artists. In 1918 he was asked by the Prime Minister of France to make a series of huge waterlily paintings to line the wall of the Orangerie building in Paris. He spent most of the last eight years of his life on this project, producing work of magnificent calm, bordering on abstract art. He died in 1926 at

Above: Waterlilies (1907), by Monet.
Below: Waterlilies (1918-26), painted for the Orangerie in Paris.

the grand old age of 86 – and over fifty years after the exhibition of 1874, which had launched Impressionism onto a startled world.

Renoir

Pierre-Auguste Renoir was one of the leading figures of the Impressionist movement, and probably became the best known of all the Impressionists in his lifetime. Back in 1869, he played a key role in establishing the Impressionist style, and he was a central participant in the Impressionist exhibitions. After living in poverty for many of these years, he became more successful in the late 1870s, and his work began to sell well.

After Impressionism

By about 1880, Renoir felt he had taken Impressionism as far as he could, and that it was time to move on. He never entirely abandoned the Impressionist technique of painting rapidly, with dabs of colour. But he began to experiment, first with more solid areas of dark colour – especially after a trip to Italy in 1881-2 – and then with more feathery brushstrokes.

Above all, though, his subject matter shifted. During the main Impressionist years of the 1870s, he painted landscapes, but also scenes of Parisian life – people at leisure, in the cafés, dancing. He also painted portraits and nudes. From the 1880s he began to concentrate on nudes, often seen bathing, painted in soft, rosy tones. He was fascinated by the play of light

Above left: Woman's Torso in the Sunlight (c.1876).

Above: Young Woman Seated (1896).

Right: The Large Tree: Woman with Red Blouse in the Garden at Cagnes (1910-12). This painting shows many features of the Impressionist style that he had developed back in the 1860s.

on skin. Sometimes he used thinner, dryer layers of paint, producing a more sketchy, scratchy effect, as seen in *Young Woman Seated*.

Pretty art

Renoir tended to paint pretty subjects, such as sweet pictures of children, including his own three sons. Many of his figures have full, round faces and fleshy cheeks, painted in the bright tones of his 'rainbow palette'. When he was criticised for this, he replied: 'Why shouldn't art be pretty? There are enough unpleasant things in the world'. His approach may have been influenced by one of his first jobs back in the 1850s, painting pictures onto pottery.

In any case, he always had a strong belief that painting was first and foremost a handicraft, to be approached like a craftsman.

Illness was one of the unpleasant things Renoir had to suffer. During the 1890s, his muscles and joints began to be affected by the painful disorder called rheumatism, and in 1903 he moved to the south of France, where the warm weather was better for his health. But he continued painting, and even began doing sculpture, with the help of assistants. He died in 1919, aged 78.

Renoir produced over 6,000 paintings – an average of about 100 a year throughout his working life.

Photographic Influences

For many centuries, artists used a piece of equipment called a camera obscura (dark box) which could project the image of the scene outside it onto a blank bit of paper. The question was: how could you capture this image to make a permanent picture? The answer lay in light-sensitive chemicals, and this is what the French scientist Joseph Nicéphore Niépce discovered when he made the very first permanent photograph in 1827.

Photomania

By the 1840s the early pioneers of photography were producing some remarkably good results. Their equipment was heavy and cumbersome and the developing processes were slow and messy, but the technology was improving all the time. By the 1860s professional photographers were setting up portrait studios in just about every town across Europe. They made inexpensive photos of people, printed on small pieces of card the size of a business card. These were so popular they became a craze, called 'cartomania'.

Some people also bought their own cameras, to pursue photography as a hobby. This became much easier in 1888, when flexible film was invented (to replace glass slides), and the rolls of film could be sent away for developing. Colour photography first became practical after about 1903.

Renoir (seated) and the French poet Stéphane Mallarmé, photographed (1895), by Degas. The paintings and drawings of Degas show the strong influence of photography, noticeable particularly in his composition.

22

A world of photography

As the old saying goes, 'The camera never lies'. It is true that photographers can select their subjects; they can choose which photographs to print and publish. But the camera simply records what is before it, unlike artists, who interpret what they see as they design and make their paintings.

Seeing the world

Photography spread rapidly around the world in the 19th century. Photographic studios were set up in Cairo, Delhi, Jakarta, Los Angeles, everywhere. Suddenly it became much easier to have believable images of people and places from around the world. It was possible, for instance, for Europeans to glimpse how others lived in places like India. Photography helped to open the eyes of the public to the whole world.

**Above right: Teatime in India.
Above: A wedding scene shows the high style of life led by Europeans in the colonies.**

Photography and art

People quickly realised that photography was not simply a matter of recording what you could see. It could also be used as an art form. The English photographer Julia Margaret Cameron (1815-79) showed how artistic choices could be introduced into portrait photographs. Photography therefore quickly became an art form in its own right.

Painters realised that they now had to do something different with their paintings – to add something that photography could not do.

Alice Liddell, the original Alice in Wonderland, photographed by Julia Margaret Cameron.

Japonisme

In 1854 Japan was forced to open its doors to foreign trade, ending over 200 years of isolation. Japan rapidly began to develop its trade and to modernise its industries. In 1862 the Japanese sent an exhibit to the London International Exhibition, and caused a sensation. European artists suddenly saw a new and exciting way of looking at and depicting the world – a vision that was expressed particularly well in the Japanese prints by artists like Hokusai.

The Japanese craze

Before long, Japanese things had become fashionable in Paris and London. People began to decorate their homes in a Japanese style, adorning them with fans, paper lanterns, prints and vases. The craze became known as 'Japonisme'. One of its greatest enthusiasts was the American painter James Abbot McNeill Whistler (1834-1903), who lived in Paris and London and studied under Gleyre in the 1850s.

Japanese objects can be seen in many paintings of interiors of this era, for example the screen and print in Manet's portrait of the French novelist Émile Zola. But the Japanese influence went deeper than this. European artists were fascinated by the surprising off-centre compositions found in Japanese prints, the use of bold patterning and blocks of colour, and also the empty spaces or 'voids'. The influence of Japanese composition is found particularly in the work of Edgar Degas.

Symphony in White No. 2: Little White Girl, painted by Whistler in 1864. The influence of Japanese art is obvious in the fan and the vase. But the unusual design of the picture, with the figure pushed to one side and a black fireplace in the centre, also echoes the off-centre compositions of Japanese prints.

Around the World
Japan

Japan has a long tradition of art and handicrafts. This can be seen in all kinds of Japanese products, such as vases, ivory carvings, lacquer boxes, fans, kimonos (the traditional form of clothing) and screens. Until the 1860s, they were hand-produced on a craft basis, but suddenly the new, foreign demand for Japanese goods encouraged manufacturers to produce many of these items on an industrial scale.

Export wares

By the 1870s, huge quantities of Japanese goods were being shipped to Europe and the USA, most of them made especially for export. They included large Imari vases, suits of samurai armour and bamboo furniture. Japanese woodblock prints also accompanied the shipments.

This new trade had a significant effect on Japanese art, and many aspects of Japanese culture were influenced by Western trends. Vases made for export, for example, became more heavily decorated, with elaborate pictures of Japanese scenes on the sides. As Japanese city-dwellers adopted Western-style clothes, there was a dramatic decline in trade for the makers of kimonos.

In Europe, on the other hand, many of the china manufacturers responded to the fashion for Japanese design by producing their own imitations of Japanese goods, such as bowls, vases and tea sets.

Imari ware container with lid, from the Edo period (c.1615–1868).

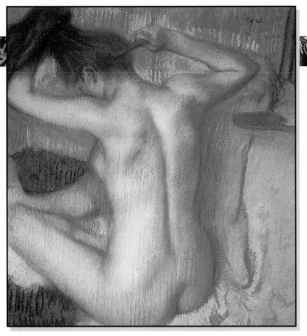

Degas

A number of artists were closely associated with the Impressionists, knew them as friends and even showed pictures in their exhibitions – but were not themselves Impressionists. One of the most celebrated of these was the French painter Edgar Degas (1834-1917). Unlike the Impressionists, he did not paint outside, and was not much interested in catching the passing moods of landscape. All his work shows a remarkable and original sense of design, influenced by both Japanese art and photography.

An eye for design

Degas' compositions look wonderfully casual. In *At the Races: Gentlemen Jockeys* there is a horse cantering in from the left, a man half out of the picture on the right, and the jockeys and horses in the centre obscure one another. More traditional painters would have tried to sort all this out into a more formal composition. It looks like a snapshot (although snapshots were not really possible until 1888). However, the way that Degas worked, in his studio, meant that his compositions were in fact meticulously planned.

At the Races: Gentlemen Jockeys (c.1877-80), by Degas.

The racecourse was one of his favourite subjects. So too were women seen in their private moments, bathing, combing their hair. Again, this went against tradition. In the past, nudes were generally shown in carefully posed compositions. Degas, on the other hand, shows women doing ordinary, everyday things, behaving just as they might when no one else is around.

Degas often worked in pastels, as opposed to oil paint, especially after his eyesight began to fail in the 1880s. Pastels are sticks of soft coloured chalks. Sold in boxes in many shades of colours, they are applied dry, directly onto paper, rather like a crayon. They can make strong lines of pure colour. The lines can also be smudged with the fingers or a rag to make areas of flat colour, and this technique can be used to mix colour and produce shading. Very rough-surfaced paper is often used for pastel, because this can produce an attractive grainy effect, called 'scruffing'.

He brings this same approach to another of his favourite themes: ballet dancers. In *Ballet: L'Étoile* the dancer is shown from a very unusual angle, as if from a theatre box. This means that we also catch a glimpse of the director, and the other dancers in the wings, waiting to come on. Again, this looks like a snapshot: the composition has been carefully designed to look as though it has not been composed at all. In other ballet pictures, Degas shows the dancers in their off-stage moments, tying up their shoes, rehearsing – more visions of a private, behind-the-scenes world.

Degas was virtually blind for the last 20 years of his life, but at his death in 1917, he was still recognised as one of the greatest artists of the 19th century.

Top left: Ballet: L'Étoile (1876-7), a pastel drawing.

Above: Detail from La Coiffure (c.1892-6). The full range of pastel techniques can be seen here. There are grainy, scruffed lines on the table, unmixed lines of colour in the clothing, and heavily mixed colour in the hair, providing a solid area of opaque colour. Degas has used a fawn-tinted paper, which provides a ready-made background colour.

Cézanne

Another artist closely associated with the Impressionists, but not one of them, was the French painter Paul Cézanne. He exhibited his work in the first Impressionist exhibition in 1874. But he soon developed his own, highly individual approach to art. He felt that it was not enough to record and copy nature. Art demanded something more: an artistic arrangement, to try to create the perfect composition. In pursuing this goal, he developed a new way of looking at the world which proved a huge influence on the next generation of artists. For this reason he is sometimes called the 'father of modern art'.

Shapes in nature

Even in his paintings made during the heyday of the Impressionist era, such as *Landscape Near Pontoise*, it is clear that Cézanne was not interested in the same effects as the Impressionists. He used massive slabs of colour rather than dabs of paint. And there are already signs of themes that would later come to preoccupy him: the shapes in the landscape, the very structure of nature. The trees, the grass in the foreground, the rectangular shapes of the buildings have been put together rather like the shaped blocks in a wooden puzzle.

Cézanne was a loner, known for his quick temper and sometimes odd behaviour. He was born into a wealthy family from Aix-en-Provence,

Peaches and Pears (1890-4), by Cézanne, one of his many carefully arranged still lifes.

and did not need to sell his paintings to survive. Cézanne's family wealth allowed him to pursue his artistic goals in isolation, rarely exhibiting his work. His first solo exhibition took place in 1895, when he was in his fifties, and he only gained full recognition right at the end of his life, a few years before his death in 1906.

Mont Sainte-Victoire, Seen from Bibémus (1897). He painted this mountain repeatedly in the last 20 years of his life.

Composition

After his move from Paris in 1886 Cézanne spent most of his life in and around Aix-en-Provence. He wanted to create the perfect composition, a picture with balance and consistency. He attempted this by carefully arranging still lifes, and then adjusting the colours – often using complementary colours – to bring about the effect that he wanted.

He came to realise that landscape also could be broken down into fairly geometric blocks of colour. At the same time, he also managed to inject an unusual sense of vibrancy, air and light into his landscapes.

This can be seen in the many pictures that he made of Mont Sainte-Victoire. He painted these en plein air, a habit shared with the Impressionists, but he had drifted well away from their goals. He wanted to turn Impressionism into something grander, more lasting, more Classical. This is why he is usually called a 'Post-Impressionist' – following on from Impressionism.

Cézanne often reworked his still lifes for so long that the fruit had rotted and shrivelled before he finished.

29

Pointillism

In the 1880s the French painters Georges Seurat (1859-91) and Paul Signac (1863-1935) took Impressionism one step further. They applied scientific ideas about colour and vision to create pictures composed entirely of tiny, regular dots of colour. Their movement was called 'Neo-Impressionism' or 'Pointillism'. For a while it was considered the most modern and daring of all the art styles.

Bathers at Asnières (1883-4), by Seurat.

Painting with dots

Seurat wanted to discover the scientific basis for the success of the Impressionists' technique, and experimented with dots of colour, seeing how the eye perceived them, blurred them and mixed them. He met Signac in 1884, and they worked closely together. Both were also involved in the creation of a new, alternative exhibition called the Salon des Indépendants, held in Paris each

year, in which anyone could show their work in return for a fee. It became the main showcase for new artists.

Seurat went on to develop other theories about painting, for example, the way that emotions are triggered by upward or downward lines. But he died suddenly, perhaps from meningitis, at the age of 31. Signac now became the leader of the movement. He continued to paint in a Pointillist style well into the 20th century, using an increasingly vibrant range of colours, and rectangular dots as opposed to round ones.

Pointillism was a very methodical and laborious way of painting, requiring great patience. In practice, Pointillism was less good at conveying movement and suited subjects that were essentially still. *Bathers at Asnières*, one of Seurat's first major Pointillist pieces, is a famous example. A very large painting, measuring about three metres wide by two metres tall, it gives a powerful impression of a hot summer's day on the River Seine.

On the one hand, such paintings have a timeless, monumental feel to them. On the other, the technique – practised largely in the studio – lacks all the spontaneous liveliness of Impressionism, and artists soon began to see its limitations.

The Pointillist palette

The Pointillist technique was based on scientific theories about vision. Seurat liked to use only the colours of the spectrum (as found in a rainbow); and, like the Impressionists, the Pointillists avoided black. They often used complementary colours next to each other (blue with orange, or red with green, or yellow with purple), to produce a vibrancy. The small dots of pure colour are quite visible close up, but from a distance the eye blurs and mixes the colours, giving the impression of a smooth, rather velvety area of one colour. The smaller the dots, the smoother this effect, and the sharper the lines.

Detail from The Harbour at Port-en-Bessin, High Tide (1888), by Seurat, showing the dotting technique, and the use of complementary colours.

Van Gogh

In the Post-Impressionist era, painting went in a number of different directions. Cézanne searched for the underlying shapes in nature and struggled to find balance in composition. The Pointillists tried to apply the science of colour and optics to painting. The Dutch painter Vincent van Gogh (1853-90) depicted his private world with a passionate, emotional intensity that reflected his mental instability. His paintings have great charm, but are haunted by his tragic tale. Today van Gogh is one of the world's most famous artists, but in his lifetime he was ridiculed and ignored.

Southern light

Van Gogh was brought up in the Netherlands, and trained as an art dealer in The Hague and London. He then went to work in a bleak mining region of Belgium, where he began to paint and draw the miseries of the poor workers' lives, in dingy colours. In 1886 he went to Paris and here he came into contact with the Impressionists. Now his work brightened up as he adopted Impressionist and Pointillist techniques. But the real change came in February 1888 when he went to live in Arles in southern France. He was amazed by the rich sunlight and warmth of the south and, now aged 34, began to develop his own distinctive style using thick brushstrokes laden with bright paint.

Van Gogh produced 420 paintings in the last two and a half years of his life. He sold just one painting in his whole lifetime.

Above: Vincent's Chair with Pipe (1888), painted at Arles.
Right: Vase with Sunflowers (1888).

Descent into nightmare

Van Gogh was already showing signs of mental illness, but he continued working at a feverish pace. In October 1888, his friend the painter Paul Gauguin came to stay with him. Two months later, they had a violent dispute, and van Gogh cut off a piece of his own left ear in frustration. In May 1889, he was admitted to a mental asylum at Saint-Rémy, near Arles, and stayed a year there.

His paintings reflected his mental turmoil, in their urgent, swirling brushstrokes. Clouds, trees and grasses look as if they, too, are filled with this emotion, an effect that is both exhilarating and threatening.

In May 1890 van Gogh went back north and stayed with his patron, the kindly psychiatrist Dr Paul Gachet, at Auvers-sur-Oise, near Paris. But in a state of acute depression in July, at the age of 37, he shot himself in a field, and died two days later.

Only after his death did the art world notice van Gogh. The Impressionists had tried to record what they saw: van Gogh painted what he felt, and this high state of emotion jumps out of his work, even when he is painting simple things. Beyond this, he had a superb gift for colour and composition, which he applied in a unique way.

Van Gogh's work was hugely influential on the development of art in the 20th century. He also cut a new figure in art: a heroic, tormented loner, living and dying for his work.

Above: Terrace of the Café at the Place du Forum in Arles in the Evening (1888).

Left: Mountainous Landscape Behind the Hospital of Saint-Rémy, painted by van Gogh in 1889.

33

Gauguin

Despite their dramatic falling-out in 1888, Paul Gauguin (1848-1903) and Vincent van Gogh had much in common. Both were struggling artists, and both were trying to find their own individual styles in the Post-Impressionist world. Gauguin ended up with rather different solutions. He used areas of flat colour and strong outlines, rather like Japanese woodcuts. But he only really found his voice by leaving France and travelling to the tropical islands of French Polynesia, in the middle of the South Pacific Ocean. Like van Gogh, he struggled with poverty and illness, and died before his talent was properly recognised.

Island dreams

Gauguin did not start his career as a painter, but as a sailor in the merchant navy and then as a stockbroker in Paris. Married and with children, he took up painting as a hobby in about 1870. He met Pissarro in 1874 and fell in with the Impressionists, exhibiting in their last four exhibitions. In 1883 he gave up his job to make painting his career, but struggled to find buyers. Nonetheless, committed to his art, he abandoned his family and went to live among a group of artists at Pont-Aven, Brittany. Here he began to develop his distinctive technique, seen, for example, in *The Yellow Christ*. The figures and trees have become stylised, almost naïve (childlike), and colour has been applied in blocks, in the manner of

The Mountain is Near (1892).

stained glass, or Japanese woodblock prints. This represents a great departure from the Impressionist style.

In 1891 he sailed to Tahiti in French Polynesia. There he found love among the Tahitian women, and led a simple life, painting

Around the World
Pacific islands

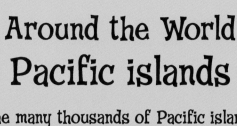

The many thousands of Pacific islands are divided into three main groups: Melanesia, Micronesia and Polynesia. Ancestors of the people living on the islands reached them in boats starting originally from South-East Asia.

Ancestors and nature

The cultures of the Pacific islands share many common themes, such as a reverence for nature, and a belief in the spiritual power of tribal ancestors. Their art was closely related to religious beliefs. It took the form of carvings and masks used in religious ceremonies, and also ordinary day-to-day objects such as boats and bowls. Some of these were collected by Europeans in the 19th century and preserved in museums. But Christian missionaries discouraged this non-Christian form of art so much of it was destroyed.

Polynesian stilt step, (late 18th-early 19th century).

vigorously and making sculptures. Now his work took on a new kind of poetry, full of exotic mystery, tropical warmth and visual beauty. He loved this life, but he was very poor, and soon became ill. In 1893 he went back to France where he recovered. He returned to French Polynesia in 1895, and lived in poverty again, often using sacking instead of canvas. He continued to work despite deteriorating health, until his death – lonely, frustrated and unrecognised – on the island of Hiva Oa in 1903. He became famous only through an exhibition of his work at the Autumn Salon in Paris in 1906.

Tahitian Woman with Fruit (1893).

Toulouse-Lautrec

Another leading figure of the Post-Impressionist era was the French painter Henri de Toulouse-Lautrec (1864-1901). He is associated mainly with Paris, and with the world of pleasure centring on the bars, cafés, dance halls, theatres, circuses, racetracks and brothels. He is also famous for his advertising posters, which have come to symbolise Paris in the 1890s. Arriving in Paris in 1885, aged 21, he met with Manet, van Gogh and Gauguin. Degas had a particularly strong influence on his work, but nonetheless his style is entirely his own.

Paintings from the underworld

Toulouse-Lautrec was born into an old aristocratic family descended from the Counts of Toulouse. He might have led a life as a country gentlemen, but two childhood accidents left him with tiny stunted legs. Seeking fulfilment in another avenue, he turned to painting.

He was a naturally gifted draughtsman, with a highly original sense of design that was clearly influenced by Japanese prints and photography. His drawing tends to take priority in his work: colour comes second. He used oil paints and pastels, and sometimes both together, with the oil thinned with turpentine to give a streaky, pastel-like effect. He often worked at high speed, leaving the finished painting or drawing sketchy.

Salon in the Rue des Moulins (1894).

Much of his work also sparkles with wit, and often pokes gentle fun at the characters he portrays.

Toulouse-Lautrec also produced a large number of prints and posters by lithography, and he became one of the great masters of

Lithography

Lithography means printing by stone (from the Greek lithos, meaning stone). The technique is based on the simple principle that water and grease do not mix. A design is drawn onto a flat surface (originally a smooth block of limestone) with a greasy wax crayon. Then the stone is covered with a layer of water. One colour of ink is applied to the stone, but it will only stick to the places where there are crayon marks. By placing paper over the stone, the ink can be printed onto it, in the shape of the wax design. Another stone is used for another part of the design, to take a different colour of ink. Slowly a picture is built up, using a series of different colours. For the *Reine de Joie* poster (left), Toulouse-Lautrec used four colours.

Toulouse-Lautrec filled his pockets with old tooth brushes. He used them to apply ink to his lithographic stones, to create a grainy effect.

the technique. Previously posters tended to be dominated by lettering: their main job was to convey information. Toulouse-Lautrec upgraded posters into a form of artistic expression. Lithography suited his style, mixing clever drawing with simplified areas of colour and startling design, combined with an inventive use of lettering. It is in his posters that the influence of Japanese design is at its strongest.

Toulouse-Lautrec's physical disabilities made him into something of a social outcast. He became a familiar figure in just the kind of low-life haunts that he liked to paint. He drank heavily, and even kept a miniature bottle of brandy and a glass hidden inside his walking stick. Despite this, he was a hard worker and a committed craftsman. But his lifestyle eventually led to a breakdown in 1899, and then an early death at the age of just 36.

Symbolism

In 1886 another very different movement was launched with a manifesto (a declaration of intentions) in a French newspaper. Called Symbolism, it covered a very broad spectrum of painters (as well as writers and musicians), working in a wide range of styles. They all rejected Realism, wanting instead to explore the world of the imagination, a world in which images could act as symbols of emotions and feelings. Many of the leading artists of the last two decades of the 19th century were associated with the Symbolist movement, including Gauguin.

Painting feelings

'Paint not the thing, but the feeling it produces', wrote the French Symbolist poet Stéphane Mallarmé (pictured on page 22). He was describing how Symbolist poets should write, but he could equally have been talking about music or painting.

Artists brought their own distinctive styles to this task. Gustave Moreau (1826-98), one of the leading French Symbolist painters, used his own streaky, feathery style to recreate a world of lost civilisations. His *Salome* series focuses on the Biblical story of the woman who persuaded King Herod to bring her the head of John the Baptist.

Fernand Khnopff (1858-1921), by contrast, used quite a realistic style to depict a dreamlike world, inhabited by hybrid animals, half-human, half-beast. Khnopff was from Belgium, where the Symbolist movement was particularly strong.

The Apparition (Salome) (1874), by Moreau.

Dream moods

Another leading figure among the French Symbolists was Odilon Redon (1840-1916), who used a soft style and golden colours, in oil and pastel, to create dreamy, flower-strewn images from myth. Redon led a reclusive life, initially drawing only in black and white.

In earlier times, it had been very hard to become a recognised artist in France without a formal training. Gauguin, for example, found it hard to gain recognition because of this attitude. But the Salon des Indépendants now allowed anyone to exhibit, which gave encouragement to all painters.

One of the most famous self-taught artists of this time was a customs official (douanier) called Henri Rousseau (1844-1910). He started painting when he was 40, and used a very polished but naïve style to create dreamy and mysterious images, often of jungle scenes inspired by his visits to the botanical gardens in Paris. Rousseau lived in great poverty after he gave up his job to paint in 1893, and often had to put up with ridicule. He had little public success until the last five or so years of his life, when his work became widely admired for its innocent charm.

Above: The Cyclops (c.1898-1900), by Redon. Normally images of the giant Polyphemus, the Cyclops, are terrifying, but here Redon makes the one-eyed monster look rather sympathetic as he approaches the object of his love, the sleeping nymph Galatea. But there is an underlying tension in the scene: it is not clear what Polyphemus will do next.

Right: Horse attacked by a Jaguar (1910), by 'Le Douanier' Rousseau. Rousseau often worked on a fairly large scale: this painting is 1.2 metres wide.

A Lady Having Tea (1893), by Denis.

Nabis

In 1888, during the Symbolist era, a small group of French artists formed a secret society in Paris called the Nabis. They included Maurice Denis (1870-1943), Pierre Bonnard (1867-1947) and Édouard Vuillard (1868-1940). Inspired by Gauguin's work in Brittany, their aim was to create a new kind of art by rejecting the realism of Impressionism and reviewing the way three-dimensional images could be created on a flat surface. In some ways, they shared the same goal as Cézanne, but their results were very different.

Decorative art

Another inspiration for the group was a painting by Paul Sérusier (1865-1927) called *Landscape: the Bois d'Amour*, also known as *The Talisman*. Virtually abstract, the artists felt that it somehow pointed to the future of art. Denis, one of the leading Symbolists, put it like this: 'A picture – before being a horse, a nude or an anecdotal (story-based) subject – is essentially a flat surface covered with colours arranged in a certain order'.

Although this seemed to suggest abstract art, that development lay some way off in the future. The Nabis stuck to figurative painting. But they explored new ways to paint on a flat surface, to create a pleasing decorative effect. In other words, they were rearranging what they saw on the canvas in a way that was primarily about shapes and colours, not the subject matter itself.

Public Gardens: Cross-Examination (1894), by Vuillard.

Art Nouveau

In 1893, the Belgian architect Victor Horta designed the Tassel House in Brussels. It was the first house built in a style which became known as Art Nouveau ('New Art'). By 1900 Art Nouveau had spread right across Europe – from Paris to St. Petersburg – and to the USA as well.

Czechoslovakia

Art Nouveau used shapes inspired by nature, such as plants and stars, to create sensual, curving designs. It bore no direct relation to any previous design style. The greatest poster designer of the Art Nouveau era was the Czech-born artist Alphonse Mucha (1860-1939), who worked in Paris and the USA before returning to Czechoslovakia in 1922.

A poster (1896), by Mucha, advertising a play starring Sarah Bernhardt, the most famous French actress of the Art Nouveau era.

Sérusier and Denis produced work that had a religious or spiritual quality. Bonnard and Vuillard used painterly Post-Impressionist styles to create harmonious images of interiors, filling the canvas with busy colour and a sense of air and light. The Nabis also produced posters, stained glass and book illustrations. The movement lasted only until the end of the 1890s, but all the participants lived on for several decades.

France-Champagne (1890), lithograph poster by Bonnard. Mirroring the happy spirit of Paris in the 1890s, this was the first work that Bonnard was able to sell.

41

Sculpture

A number of artists of the Post-Impressionist era tried their hands at sculpture, including Degas and Gauguin. Degas produced a number of small pieces, notably of dancers and horses, especially after his eyesight began to fail in the 1890s. But the sculptor who towered over all others was Auguste Rodin (1840-1917), who was also French. He brought a Realist's eye to his work, and reproduced the human body with such accuracy that some people thought he must be secretly making casts from live human beings. He transformed French sculpture, which had become stuck in a watered-down Classical tradition.

Real people

Rodin's sculptures caused a considerable stir. His marble statue called *The Kiss*, showing a naked couple kissing, was dismissed as pornographic by some. Yet it was in many ways simply a modern version of the kind of sculpture made by ancient Greek and Roman sculptors, which were so widely admired by art lovers. Another of his famous sculptures was *The Thinker*.

Rodin's sculpture seems new, modern and fresh because he did not attempt to make idealised versions of the human form. His figures look like real people. But Rodin was not simply copying direct from life. His figures have an impressive and poetic grace to them. He often also emphasised their sculptural quality by leaving parts of the work unfinished – just as Michelangelo had done some 400 years earlier.

The Thinker (1889-1906), by Rodin.

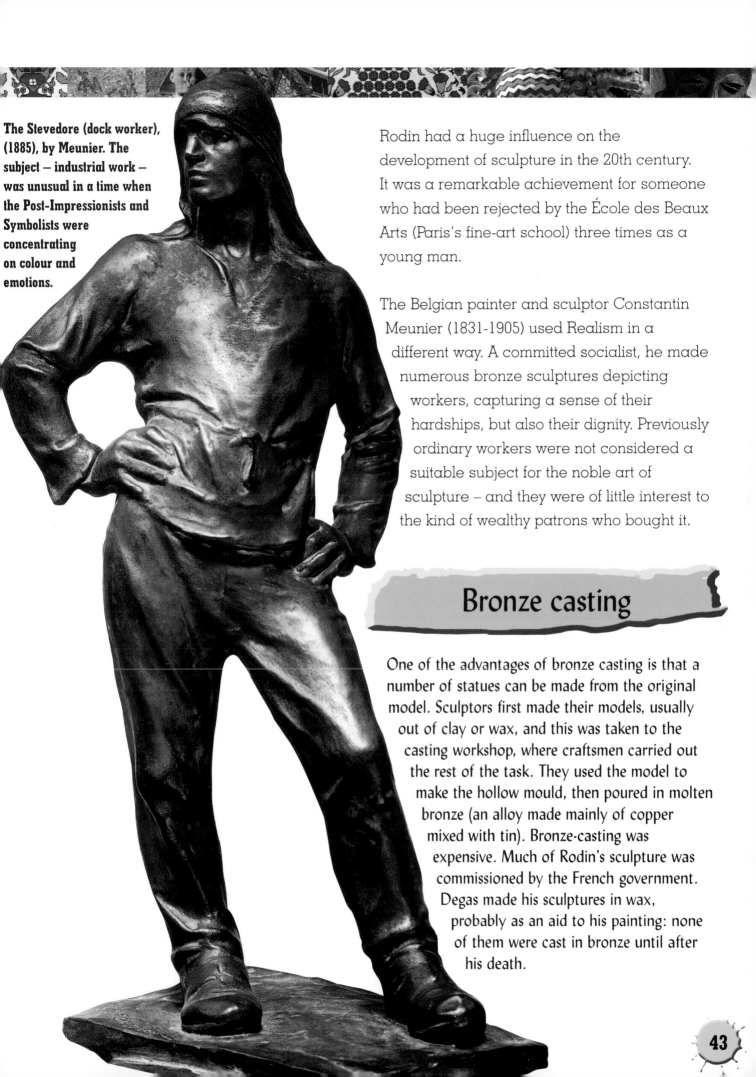

The Stevedore (dock worker), (1885), by Meunier. The subject – industrial work – was unusual in a time when the Post-Impressionists and Symbolists were concentrating on colour and emotions.

Rodin had a huge influence on the development of sculpture in the 20th century. It was a remarkable achievement for someone who had been rejected by the École des Beaux Arts (Paris's fine-art school) three times as a young man.

The Belgian painter and sculptor Constantin Meunier (1831-1905) used Realism in a different way. A committed socialist, he made numerous bronze sculptures depicting workers, capturing a sense of their hardships, but also their dignity. Previously ordinary workers were not considered a suitable subject for the noble art of sculpture – and they were of little interest to the kind of wealthy patrons who bought it.

Bronze casting

One of the advantages of bronze casting is that a number of statues can be made from the original model. Sculptors first made their models, usually out of clay or wax, and this was taken to the casting workshop, where craftsmen carried out the rest of the task. They used the model to make the hollow mould, then poured in molten bronze (an alloy made mainly of copper mixed with tin). Bronze-casting was expensive. Much of Rodin's sculpture was commissioned by the French government. Degas made his sculptures in wax, probably as an aid to his painting: none of them were cast in bronze until after his death.

Anticipation of Expressionism

Van Gogh filled many of his paintings with passionate feeling. By abandoning realism in favour of raw emotion, his work was anticipating a movement of the early 20th century, called Expressionism. But he was not alone in this. Several other painters trod a similar path. One of the most curious is the Belgian-English painter James Ensor (1860-1949). Early in his career he mastered the technique of Impressionism, and produced some fine interiors and portraits in about 1880-2. Then his subject matter became increasingly personal and bizarre.

Masks and emotions

By the mid-1880s, Ensor was depicting strange scenes involving battling skeletons, dead fish and nightmarish groups of masked characters. He used thick brushstrokes heavily laden with paint, and areas of vivid and clashing colour – pure reds and greens. There is an obsessive quality to his work, fascinating, humorous and disturbing. In his great masterpiece, the large *Entry of Christ into Brussels* (1888), he pokes fun at Belgian society and the Church. Caricatured dignitaries, painted in a crude, naïve style, jostle for space in a parade, with Jesus virtually obscured, bringing up the rear. It caused an uproar. Ensor was asked to leave the fashionable modern art club called Les Vingt in Brussels, and he became a recluse, living most of the rest of his life in his home town, the North Sea port of Ostend.

Self-Portrait with Masks (1899), by Ensor. Ensor appears like an island of reason and normality as a nightmarish crowd of grotesque masks presses around him.

The Scream (1893), by Munch. This is one of several versions that Munch made of the same subject, reflecting his own mental torment. He wrote: 'I stood there trembling with fear, and I felt a loud, unending scream piercing nature'.

When Munch's work was shown at an exhibition in Berlin in 1892, it provoked such blazing criticism in the press that the exhibition was forced to close.

Ensor's obsession with masks can partly be explained by the fact that his parents sold carnival masks in their novelty shop in Ostend. Even as a grown man he remained surrounded by the odd mixture of objects of the kind portrayed in *Still Life with Masks*. He was one of the first European painters to take an interest in African masks – which became a key source of inspiration to artists such as Picasso in the early 20th century.

More influential still was the Norwegian painter Edvard Munch (1863-1944). After a disturbed childhood, during which his mother and sister died of tuberculosis, he took up painting, and travelled to Paris in the 1880s. There he was inspired by the Impressionists, the Symbolists, by the work of Gauguin and, later, by van Gogh. But his style of painting was frenzied, conveying his deep emotional turmoil. Munch lived mainly in Berlin from 1892 to 1908. During this time he worked on a huge project called the *Frieze of Life* ('a poem of life, love and death'). His most famous

painting, *The Scream*, was part of this series. In 1908, however, he suffered a mental breakdown and returned to live in Norway. He realised that the emotion he put into his work was partly responsible for his mental instability, and from now on he painted gentler, brighter and more positive subjects.

But it is *The Scream* that everyone remembers – a deeply haunting picture, in which the entire landscape seems to be conspiring to torment and crush the central character, provoking a wail of anguish. The vigour of the work, the simplicity of the composition and the crude use of colour and paint show a new freedom of expression which was to become a key theme in art in the following century.

Chronology of the Impressionist Era

1827 Nicéphore Niépce makes the first permanent photograph.

1849 Death of Hokusai, master of Japanese woodblock prints.

1851 Death of J.M.W. Turner.

1854 Japan ends its isolation, and opens its doors to trade.

1855 Courbet mounts his *Réalisme* exhibition in Paris.

1862 A Japanese exhibit at the London International Exhibition triggers the Japanese influence in Western art.

1863 Manet's *Déjeuner sur l'Herbe* causes a scandal at the Salon des Refusés.

1864 Closure of Charles Gleyre's art school, where several Impressionists were taught.

1874 First Impressionist exhibition in Paris: the name 'Impressionism' is coined by a hostile critic.

1876-77 Monet paints his *Gare Saint-Lazare* series.

1884 Seurat completes *Bathers at Asnières*, his first major Pointillist work.

1886 The term 'Pointillism' is coined. Symbolism is officially launched.

1888 Van Gogh settles in Arles, in the South of France. The Nabis are formed.

1890 Van Gogh commits suicide.

1891 Gauguin travels to Tahiti. Monet exhibits his *Haystacks* series.

1893 Munch paints *The Scream*.

1901 Death of Toulouse-Lautrec.

1906 Gauguin's work is shown to great acclaim in Paris, three years after his death.

1918 Monet begins his final great project, *Waterlilies*, for the Orangerie, Paris.

1919 Death of Renoir.

1926 Death of Monet.

A brief history of art

The earliest known works of art are small carved figurines dating from 30,000 BC. Cave painting dates back to 16,000 BC. Sculpture was the great art form of Ancient Greece, from about 500 BC. Greek sculptors attempted to make brilliantly lifelike images.

In Europe, the Renaissance began in the 1300s when artists in Italy rediscovered the culture of the ancient Romans and Greeks. Renaissance artists include painters such as **Giotto** (c.1267-1337), **Masaccio** (1401-28), **Leonardo da Vinci** (1452-1519) and **Jan van Eyck** (c.1390-1441). **Michelangelo Buonarroti** (1475-1564) made sculpture as fine as anything the Romans or Greeks had produced.

In Europe, Mannerist painters such as **El Greco** (1541-1614) were beginning to put emotion into their paintings. Painters of the Baroque period, such as **Pieter-Paul Rubens** (1577-1640), displayed dazzling technical skill and a sense of glamour. The Dutch painter **Rembrandt van Rijn** (1606-69) showed in his portraits how painting could capture the character of the sitter.

Artists could now paint detailed pictures of reality, but they found that this was not enough. Painters such as **Francisco Goya** (1746-1828) adapted their style to convey personal expression and emotion. Emotion was a key element of Romanticism. In his late work, **J. M. W. Turner** (1775-1851) used freely applied dashes of colour to convey feeling.

In the Realist movement, artists such as **Gustave Courbet** (1819-77) used their skills to portray real life. In the 1870s, the Impressionists such as **Pierre-Auguste Renoir** (1841-1919) and **Claude Monet** (1840-1926) took Realism in a new direction. They painted outdoors, and rapidly, trying to capture the passing moments of the world. The Post-Impressionists such as **Paul Gauguin** (1848-1903), **Vincent van Gogh** (1853-90) and **Paul Cézanne** (1839-1906) developed highly individual styles.

In the 20th century, a series of artists' movements followed one after the other. In Cubism, **Pablo Picasso** (1881-1973) explored new ways to look at objects. Expressionism concentrated on putting emotion into painting. The Surrealists, such as **Salvador Dali** (1904-89) and **René Magritte** (1898-1967), depicted highly imaginative, dreamlike worlds. The development of abstract art was taken a step further in the works of **Piet Mondrian** (1872-1944), while **Jackson Pollock** (1912-56) launched Abstract Expressionism. In the late 20th century Pop artists such as **Andy Warhol** (1928-87) explored the meaning of art, as did the Minimalists such as **Carl André** (1935-), and installation artists such as **Joseph Beuys** (1921-86), took art in new directions.

Glossary

Abstract art
Any form of art that does not represent things in the real world, but is composed simply of shapes or colours.

Complementary colours
Colours that appear on the opposite sides of the colour wheel, in which one primary colour faces the mixture of the two other primary colours. Complementary colours intensify one another when placed side by side.

Impasto
Oil paint applied in thick brushstrokes.

Lithography
A means of making prints, originally using a large flat stone and a wax crayon.

Plein air
French for 'open air'. A term used for the practice of making complete landscape oil paintings out of doors.

Pointillism
A painting technique, named in 1886, in which the image is built up using small, regular dots of colour.

Post-Impressionist
Any of a number of styles of the late 19th-century painting which evolved directly from Impressionism.

Realism
A term used to describe art that imitates real life and the real world, without idealising it.

Scruffing
The dotting effect seen when pastels are drawn lightly over rough-surfaced paper.

Index